Dermody Advertising

REGULATION OF
ADVERTISING BY THE FTC

Richard A. Posner

American Enterprise Institute for Public Policy Research
Washington, D.C.

Richard A. Posner is professor of law at the
University of Chicago Law School.

Evaluative Studies 11, November 1973

ISBN 0-8447-3119-6

Library of Congress Catalog Card No. L.C. 73-90481

Printed in United States of America

CONTENTS

INTRODUCTION

The Federal Trade Commission (FTC), established in 1915, is an independent federal agency with a variety of duties, including statistical reporting, safety regulation, and antitrust enforcement.[1] This study concerns only one of these duties, the regulation of advertising content. It is not a complete critique of the work of the Federal Trade Commission.

Section I analyzes false advertising in relation to the general problem of consumer information. The reason for undertaking such an analysis is that, as we shall see, Congress has not spelled out clear directions with respect to the regulation of advertising, and the FTC must therefore look to other sources for guidance in enforcement policy. Section I suggests an analytical basis for such a policy.

Section II discusses the legislative framework within which the FTC operates—the congressional mandate (such as it is) and the commission's powers, organization, and funding. As the first section is concerned with developing the ends that the commission might pursue in the regulation of advertising, so the second explains the means that are available to the commission in the pursuit of those (or other) ends.

Section III discusses the evolution of commission policy in the advertising area. It has two parts. The first considers the body of false-advertising doctrine built up by the commission over the years. This body of doctrine is examined, using a sample of commission cases decided during the 1960s. Following the appointment of Miles Kirkpatrick as chairman in 1970, the commission took a number of important initiatives—substantive, procedural, and remedial—in the advertising area. These recent developments are discussed in the second part.

A few words about two terms are in order here. First, "advertising" as used throughout this study refers to all methods by which sellers seek to inform (or misinform) consumers in order to induce them to buy products. It includes labeling, point-of-sale advertising, oral representations by salesmen, and other sales promotion techniques, as well as media advertising. False advertising would thus include virtually every use of deceptive practices in order to sell products. Second, "fraud" is used to refer to any misleading claim or omission in a seller's promotion of a product. This is a broader usage than the common law and criminal definitions of the term.

I. ADVERTISING, INFORMATION, AND FRAUD

The Production and Sale of Information

For markets to operate effectively, buyers must have accurate information about the quality and other characteristics of the products offered for sale. Otherwise there can be no basis for confidence that the market will enable consumers to make purchases maximizing their welfare within the limitations of their resources. The production of information about products is therefore of fundamental importance to the effective operation of a market system.[1]

Yet one observes relatively few entrepreneurs engaged in the production and sale of product information to consumers. This seems surprising, considering the importance of such information. The likely reason why the production of product information for sale to consumers is relatively uncommon is that property rights in information are not well developed. If A publishes information about a product in a magazine to which B subscribes, C, who hears about the information from B, will have obtained the benefits of the information without having helped A to defray the costs of producing it. A has no legal right to prevent C from using the information without A's consent, as he would have a legal right to prevent C from using his land without his consent.

The costs of enforcing elaborate property rights in information would probably be prohibitive. Whether for that or other reasons, such rights are not, in general, recognized.[2] As a result of the absence of an adequate system of property rights, the production of information for direct sale to consumers may not be carried to the point where the value of a unit of information would be just equal to its cost. Fortunately, there are other methods by which the production of consumer product information is stimulated.

The Provision of Information by Sellers

A great deal of information about products is generated by the sellers of the products and by consumers themselves. In looking to see why, it is first necessary to observe that the cost of a product to the consumer has at least two components: (1) the price charged by the seller and (2) the cost to the consumer of informing himself about (that is, finding) the product—what the economist calls the cost of search.[3] Up to a point, additional search generates price savings larger than the cost of search. Hence the consumer has an incentive to acquire knowledge about the products he buys. The seller can sometimes reduce the consumer's search cost by disseminating information about the product. Where the cost of this dissemination is less than the savings in consumer search costs, the seller can be expected to supply information: by doing so he can reduce the total cost of the product to the consumer and thereby increase the quantity of product demanded.

As a result of increases in the complexity and variety of products and in the value of people's time (time being the principal resource consumed in search), it can be surmised that there has occurred a major shift from consumer to seller in the comparative advantage of supplying consumer product information. This is apparent in the growth, for example, of methods of selling such as the department stores, which function as intermediaries between producer and consumer, certifying the quality of goods to the consumer and thereby supplying him with essential information about the goods. Today the role of information dissemination by sellers is a large one.

Deterrents to the Provision of Misleading Information by Sellers

Reliance on sellers for information about products does not provide complete assurance that the information disseminated will be truthful. The seller's general purpose is to provide information that, if believed, will induce consumers to buy his product in preference to other sellers' products. He may therefore be expected to be interested in the truth of the claims only insofar as it bears on their believability. It must be considered whether there are adequate market or legal mechanisms (apart from the type of legal regulation carried on by the Federal Trade Commission) that will deter sellers from making false claims.

There are at least four mechanisms available. The first is the knowledge and intelligence of the consumer. Many false claims would not be worth making simply because the consumer knows better than to believe them. Rising levels of education have probably reduced the credulity of the average consumer, who, without making a substantial investment in research, can doubtless see through many potential forms of dishonest advertising. This conclusion is especially convincing when one considers products that the consumer inspects or samples before purchasing. The opportunities for deception with respect to these products are negligible except where a reasonable inspection would fail to expose the falsity of the seller's claim. Misrepresentations of a cantaloupe's ripeness, the comfort of a pair of shoes, or the glitter of a necklace would rarely be attempted, because they would so rarely succeed. The composition of the shoes or of the necklace might be a different matter.[4]

The second factor that operates to discourage the making of false claims about products is the cost to a seller of developing a reputation for dishonesty. A seller cannot expect a false claim to go undetected indefinitely. If the profitability of his business depends on repeated sales to the same customers, as is true of most established sellers, a policy of false advertising is likely to be short-sighted and therefore bad business: customers will take their business elsewhere after they discover the fraud. Even if the seller does not depend on repeat customers, prospective customers may hear about his fraud from his former customers and be deterred from patronizing him. False advertising in these situations will be extremely costly to the seller in the long run.

Conversely, fraud may be attractive to two kinds of sellers. The first is one who sells a product (or service) whose effectiveness is so uncertain that consumers may not detect false claims about its performance even in the long run—as with providers of medical care. The second type of seller is one whose dependence on repeat customers, or on a good reputation generally, is so slight that he is immune to effective retaliation by former customers. A seller having no fixed business locale, no resources specialized to his current business, no visibility, no stable customer group, would be in this position. An example would be an itinerant peddler.

A third constraint on false advertising is competition. If A's competitor, B, makes a false claim designed to increase B's sales, and the claim is believed by consumers, A will lose sales to B. This will give A an incentive either to rebut B's false claims in an advertising campaign or to sue him.⁵ Three qualifications are necessary here, however.

First, A's incentive to rebut the falsity will be limited by the costs of doing so in relation to the gain from recapturing the sales lost to B. That gain may be slight if B's falsehood results in diverting to him a small number of sales from each of many competing firms (C, D, E, F, et cetera, as well as A). In these circumstances, no individual competitor will have an incentive to expend substantial sums in exposing B's fraud although the aggregate diversion of business to B, and hence the harm to consumers, may be great. The obvious solution to this problem is for the honest sellers to pool their efforts and thereby reduce the individual costs of combating the deception. Such cooperative activity is not unknown—it is in fact carried on by trade associations—but it is made less likely by the transaction costs involved in coordinating the activities of a large number of independent sellers, a factor much illuminated in the analysis of cartels.⁶

Second, A may do just as well by matching B's falsehood as by attempting to refute it. This is not always possible—B may be falsely representing that he is A! And matching may be costly to A's reputation for honest dealing. Conversely, refuting B's false claim might, by increasing A's reputation for fair dealing, enable A not only to recapture the sales lost to B but to capture additional sales from B.

Third, if an industry is highly competitive, the costs of entry into and exit from the industry tend to be low. This suggests that the penalty for a firm that develops a reputation for dishonest dealing may be smaller in highly competitive industries.

The monopolization of an industry, whether by a single firm or by a cartel of sellers, is conducive to deceptive advertising in two respects. First, the likelihood of effective customer retaliation when the fraud is unmasked is small: the customer has no close substitute to which he can turn. (This point must be balanced, however, against the point about exit costs made above.) Second, the incentive of other sellers to combat false claims is weak. A monopolist's false claim is unlikely to reduce any other seller's sales sharply. To be sure, when the demand for a monopolized industry's product increases (for whatever reason), sales of other products—substitutes for the monopolized product—will decrease. But by hypothesis there is no very close substitute for the monopolized product (otherwise there would be no monopoly), so the sales losses will be distributed among the producers of a variety of distant substitutes and no one of them will suffer a substantial loss of sales. The many who are slightly affected are unlikely to constitute a sufficiently homogeneous group to take effective collective action (through a trade association or otherwise) against the false advertiser. However, a point the other way is that the absence of close substitutes may reduce the return to false advertising: a seller has little incentive to advertise that his product is superior to competing products if there are no competing products.

The monopoly case is probably not an important one empirically. But analysis of it suggests a case that is important—where a product's misrepresented attribute is common to all of the sellers in the industry. An example is the danger to health from smoking cigarettes. If one cigarette manufacturer stated or implied that smoking his cigarettes was healthful, it would be foolish for the other manufacturers of cigarettes to reply that smoking was in fact hazardous. No cigarette manufacturer can correct the false claim without disparaging his own product. The more effective course could be to match the claim. As for other sellers, the claim that smoking is healthful may increase the sales of cigarettes at their expense, but since their products will be only distant substitutes,[7] these sellers will have little incentive to advertise that cigarettes are hazardous in order to retrieve the customers that they have lost to the cigarette industry. Nor is this a case where, once consumers have discovered the truth, they can be expected to retaliate against the deception by switching to another seller: no one sells a nonhazardous cigarette.

The cigarette case makes it clear, however, that sellers are not the only sources of product information. Disclosures of the dangers of cigarette smoking have come from other sources and have been significant factors in the production and sale of presumably safer cigarettes—filter cigarettes and cigarettes low in tar and nicotine.

The fourth deterrent to fraud that we will mention consists of private law remedies. A material misrepresentation in a consumer sale will generally constitute both a breach of contract and a tort. Frequently, to be sure, the cost of enforcing a legal claim will be greater than the value of the product or service involved in the deception. But the emergence of the consumer class action, which permits the pooling of a large number of small consumer claims, has undermined this objection to reliance on private legal remedies—assuming that recent decisions do not fatally weaken the class action remedies by putting the burden of notification of all members of the class upon the plaintiff. Moreover, a legal claim of fraud may be quite inexpensive for the consumer to prosecute if the transaction is so arranged that the burden of enforcement falls on the seller (the consumer may be refusing to complete payment under an installment sales contract, claiming that the sale was fraudulent). In some cases, in addition, an individual claim will be so large that it clearly justifies the costs of private suit. The cigarette case is an important example. The consequence of fraud with respect to the health characteristics of cigarette smoking may be death from lung cancer. If the cigarette manufacturer is liable for this consequence, the damages will be large enough to induce the injured consumer to press his claim for common law fraud.[8]

Market Characteristics Favorable to Fraud

To summarize, there are some market settings in which the problem of consumer fraud would probably not be serious even in the absence of direct governmental regulation and others where it might well be. The dangerous area includes cases where the performance of the product or service in question is highly uncertain (making false claims difficult to detect) or where the seller can terminate at low cost (making him substantially immune to customer retaliation). The first category embraces many restorative services, ranging from auto repair to medicine.[9] The second includes various "fly-by-night" operations in which the seller does not have a substantial investment that would be jeopardized if customers, having discovered the fraud being perpetrated upon them, ceased to deal with him.

Another characteristic that may predispose a market to fraud—but one that is probably not very important empirically—is monopoly. Monopoly reduces the incentive of other sellers to correct fraudulent misrepresentations and limits the customer's practical ability to retaliate after he discovers that he has been defrauded. A related but more important question is whether the product itself (as distinct from a particular seller's brand of the product) has a characteristic susceptible of being misrepresented (such as the healthfulness of smoking). If such a characteristic exists and is misrepresented by one seller, other sellers of the product will have little or no incentive to supply corrective information, since that information would reduce their sales as well as the sales of the firm making the false claim.

Also relevant to the propensity to defraud are the costs to the buyer of protecting himself against fraud, by obtaining, on his own, sufficient information about the product so as not to be dependent upon information supplied by sellers. If the costs of information to the consumer are low, a serious problem of fraud is unlikely to arise regardless of the factors discussed above. The major cost involved in a consumer's effort to inform himself about products and about alternative sellers is his time. Hence the cost of information to the consumer will depend on the amount of time that he must spend to obtain it and on the value of his time. This may seem to imply that poor people might actually be less rather than more likely than wealthy people to be defrauded. The lower value of the poor person's time reduces the cost to him of search. However, education may increase the efficiency of the search, and education and income are highly correlated. The wealthy person may search less but the time he does spend in search will tend to be more productive than the time spent by the poor person. Which effect dominates is not clear. The main point is that the conventional belief that the poor are more susceptible than other people to being defrauded does not have a firm analytical basis.

These then are the characteristics—of sellers, products, and buyers—that predispose a market to consumer fraud, that is, to a failure to supply enough truthful information about a product to enable the consumer to make the purchases that maximize his satisfactions. If these characteristics are absent, the likelihood of successful fraud is small. In competitive markets composed of sellers who have a substantial interest in maintaining reputations for fair dealing and who sell products whose performance characteristics are readily determinable by the consumer, the likelihood of significant consumer fraud is small. However, even if one finds the predisposing characteristics present, that does not conclude the analysis. It is still necessary to consider the consumer's private law remedies (which may or may not be adequate) as well as the private remedies —and incentives to pursue them—available to competitors of the dishonest seller, before concluding that direct government regulation is warranted.

Appraising Commission Activity

The discussion in this section supplies criteria for appraising the Federal Trade Commission's efforts in the false-advertising field. Has the FTC concentrated its resources in areas where consumer fraud is likely to be a serious problem? Or has it dissipated its resources in other areas? These questions will be uppermost when, in Section III of this study, the commission's activities in the consumer-fraud area are reviewed.

The answers to these questions, however, are not a sufficient basis for appraising those activities. It must also be considered whether, to the extent that the commission has devoted its resources to the prevention of substantial frauds, it has used enforcement methods reasonably designed to eliminate the frauds at acceptable cost. Before this question can be answered, more must be known about the commission's powers and procedures—which leads to Section II of this paper.

II. THE LEGISLATIVE FRAMEWORK

The Federal Trade Commission is constrained by the statutes under which it operates as well as by the resources supplied to it by Congress. The major question addressed in this section is whether the legislative framework enables the commission to deal effectively with the problems of consumer fraud identified in Section I.

Legislative Intent

The basic statute under which the commission operates is the Federal Trade Commission Act of 1914, as amended.[1] Section 5 of the act gives the commission its basic mandate. The section as originally enacted directed the FTC to prevent "unfair methods of competition" in interstate commerce. From the legislative history, it appears that by this term Congress meant anticompetitive practices and that Congress recognized the term was broad enough to include fraudulent sales practices but intended that the commission would devote most of its attention to the suppression of anticompetitive practices.[2] Indeed, so preoccupied were the framers of the act with the commission's role in supplementing antitrust enforcement that the intended role for the commission—if any—as an agency for protecting consumers against fraud (except in the unlikely circumstance in which fraud might promote monopoly) was left wholly undefined.

Nonetheless, from its earliest days the FTC devoted substantial resources to prosecuting consumer fraud cases.[3] To circumvent objections that a mandate to prevent unfair methods of competition did not include efforts to protect consumers, the commission routinely included in its fraud complaints the recital that the fraudulent

11

practice harmed the honest competitors of the defendant by diverting sales from them. Eventually, however, the Supreme Court held that, in the absence of proof of such an effect, the commission could not act against consumer fraud.[4] This decision led to proposals for amendment of the original legislation.

In 1938 Section 5 of the Federal Trade Commission Act was amended to direct the commission to prevent "unfair or deceptive acts or practices," as well as "unfair methods of competition," thereby making explicit the commission's duty to protect consumers from fraud in circumstances where no harmful effect on other sellers could be established.[5] Neither the statute nor the legislative history, however, defines "unfair or deceptive," and while congressional approval of the FTC's decision to operate in the deceptive-practices area was made clear, the permissible scope of its activities was not, nor has Congress ever clarified the matter.

The vagueness of the legislative mandate underscores the importance of the economic analysis in Section I of this study. This is not a case where the purpose of Congress in establishing a legislative program is clear and the question is whether the program has been implemented in accordance with that purpose. Congress has never furnished criteria by which the success of the commission's activities in the false-advertising area could be appraised.[6] That is why it is necessary to look elsewhere for criteria.

Jurisdiction, Procedures, and Remedies

The scope and powers of the Federal Trade Commission, in their present form, are the product of a series of amendments to the 1914 act. It is not necessary here to trace the changes in the commission's authority, only to describe that authority as it exists today.

The FTC is limited to the prevention of unfair or deceptive acts or practices "in commerce," defined as meaning commerce within the District of Columbia or interstate commerce. Thus all sellers in the District of Columbia and all sellers elsewhere who make at least some sales across state lines (or advertise in newspapers that cross state lines) are subject to the commission's jurisdiction. Virtually all sellers, except small independent (that is, nonchain) retailers, have some interstate sales and so are subject to the commission's jurisdiction.

A few businesses that operate in interstate commerce are expressly excluded from FTC jurisdiction.[7] Some businesses are included in the commission's jurisdiction by special statute whether or not they have any interstate sales—as, for example, retail sellers of furs, wool products, and textile fiber products. The substantive provisions of the statutes governing these products are discussed below.

The basic mandate of the FTC is "to prevent" deceptive practices, a phrase that suggests a certain procedural flexibility. However, the Federal Trade Commission Act itself sets out only one procedure by which the commission can act.[8] This procedure involves, as a first step, the commission's issuance of a complaint alleging that a particular seller has engaged or is engaging in a deceptive practice. The complaint is served upon the seller, who is the respondent in the proceeding. If the respondent decides to contest the complaint, the matter is set for trial before a hearing examiner — recently renamed "administrative law judge"—who is an employee of the commission but not subject to its direction and who operates much like a state or federal trial-court judge. The prosecutor at the trial is a lawyer from one of the commission's prosecutorial divisions. If at the conclusion of the trial the examiner orders the complaint dismissed, the prosecutor, or "complaint counsel," can appeal the examiner's decision to the full commission, sitting as an appellate tribunal. The respondent can likewise appeal if the examiner's decision is against him. Judicial review of the commission's decision is available in a federal court of appeals (with Supreme Court review of the court of appeals' decision by writ of certiorari). But it is available only to the respondent. Complaint counsel is not authorized to seek judicial review of a commission decision.

If the examiner, or the commission on appeal, adjudges the respondent guilty of the violation charged in the complaint, an order is entered directing the respondent to cease and desist from the unlawful conduct. A cease-and-desist order is much like an injunction. Like an injunction, it need not be wholly negative in its terms: it may spell out particular requirements that the respondent must follow. Once the cease-and-desist order has become final, either because the court of appeals has affirmed the commission or because the respondent has not sought judicial review, a subsequent violation of the order subjects the respondent to a fine of $5,000 per violation, or $5,000 a day if the violation is a continuing one. This fine—technically a civil rather than a criminal penalty—is enforced through federal court actions brought by the Department of Justice.

There are no provisions for bringing damage actions by the commission, except insofar as the civil penalty for violation of a final cease-and-desist order may be viewed as a species of damages. However, the FTC has recently asserted a limited authority to order money payments by respondents. This is discussed in Section III below.

As with judicial actions, there is provision for the settlement of commission suits without trial. In fact, consent orders to cease and desist, negotiated by complaint counsel and respondent and approved by the commission, greatly outnumber litigated cases.

From its earliest days, the commission has construed the 1914 act to permit other remedial procedures to be followed besides the one explicitly prescribed in the act. Among these are "guides" and "trade practice rules," which contain detailed interpretations of the application of the fairness standard of Section 5 of the Federal Trade Commission Act to particular advertising practices (such as the use of the term "free") or to the advertising practices of particular industries and advisory opinions, which serve the same function for existing or proposed activities of a particular company. In addition, the commission has employed less formal alternatives to consent orders like the "assurance of voluntary discontinuance," a non-binding agreement by a firm to discontinue a practice questioned by the commission's staff.

By far the most important remedial or procedural innovation of the FTC is the trade regulation rule.[9] This controversial procedure permits binding determinations of fact to be made without a trial in informal hearings resembling those conducted by congressional committees. The commission's position is that facts found in such a proceeding cannot be challenged by respondents in a subsequent action to enforce the rule.[10] The procedure thus provides a substantial shortcut to a finding of deception, especially in situations where the challenged practice is common to many firms, so that it would be costly to sue the firms individually. The commission's legal authority to issue such rules was recently upheld.[11]

The specialized statutes applicable to the fur, wool, and textile fiber industries deserve separate mention.[12] They are enforced by the same procedures used in the enforcement of the more general mandate of Section 5 of the Federal Trade Commission Act, except that the commission's rulemaking power under the specialized statutes is more explicit and has been used more frequently. Some of the flavor of the substantive provisions of these statutes and regulations will emerge in the next section. The commission has quite recently been given additional substantive authority by the Truth in Lending Act, also discussed in Section III.[13]

Adequacy of Commission Powers

The fundamental question raised here is whether the FTC has sufficient powers to deal effectively with the problems of consumer information identified in Section I. Substantively, the commission's mandate is sufficiently flexible to enable it to deal rationally with these problems. The generality of the legislative mandate would appear to leave the commission substantially free to adopt policies designed to maximize consumer welfare.

The cardinal deficiency in the legislative framework is in the area of remedies. Specifically it is the absence of any provision for money damages, compensatory or punitive. The commission's inability to award monetary reparations to victimized consumers has two effects. First, it weakens the consumer's incentive to lodge complaints of fraud with the commission. The FTC is thereby deprived of substantial private assistance in enforcing the law against deceptive selling. Second, it weakens the seller's incentive to comply with the statutes enforced by the commission. The only consequence of violation is that, if apprehended and successfully prosecuted (an outcome by no means certain), a fraudulent seller will be prevented from continuing, or repeating, the violation. (This assumes, but reasonably, that the monetary penalties for violation of an order are effective in deterring such violations.) The seller is permitted to keep any profits obtained during the period of violation. Incentive to comply with the law is especially weak among "fly-by-night" operators, an important source of fraudulent selling. Their methods of operation give them a good chance of avoiding punishment altogether, so that they have especially little to fear from merely preventive remedies.

In general, effective deterrence would seem to require a monetary penalty equal to the cost to the victims of the violations for which the wrongdoer is apprehended divided by the probability (always less than one) of apprehension and punishment.[14] The commission's inability to impose penalties so measured would seem to disable it from effectively deterring fraud.

This is not to say that FTC proceedings will have no effect whatever on a firm's incentive to attempt fraud. There are at least three reasons why there may be such an effect.

First, insofar as there is a positive probability that the commission will apprehend and enjoin unlawful conduct, the firm's return from fraud will be smaller (because received for a shorter period) than if there were no legal sanctions. To be sure, the difference may be slight, especially if (1) the commission's proceedings are protracted (but a respondent will have to incur legal expenses to protract a proceeding against it) and (2) the fraud would have been discovered anyway by customers, and therefore presumably discontinued by the firm, in not much more time than it takes the commission to enter a final order. Second, the order prevents the repetition of the unlawful conduct. The monetary penalty for violation of an order is severe, and, therefore, one assumes, effective. Third, the order will often enjoin some conduct distinct from, although related to, the precise conduct giving rise to the proceeding. But on balance the commission's sanctions seem weak.

There is an element of irony in the commission's lack of strong sanctions. The original Federal Trade Commission Act reveals an obvious willingness to trade strong sanctions for flexible procedures. The act provided virtually no sanctions[15] and exacted from the commission virtually no recognition of the procedural rights of the accused. Over time the sanctions have been strengthened, primarily by the addition of the provision for civil penalties. But the respondent's procedural rights have been strengthened even more, primarily by the enactment of the Administrative Procedure Act,[16] whose provisions are applicable to the commission. Today the commission's trial procedures are hardly distinguishable from those of an ordinary court.

As will be seen later, the Federal Trade Commission retains certain institutional characteristics that suggest it might not be well to endow it with sanctions equivalent to those of courts. The question arises whether, given the apparent incompatibility between punitive sanctions and the commission form of regulation, it is preferable that effective sanctions be forgone or that the commission form be abandoned. This question will be discussed in Section IV.

III. THE COMMISSION'S WORK PRODUCT

In almost sixty years of activity in the deceptive-practices area, the Federal Trade Commission has issued thousands of decisions, as well as a variety of rules, guides, and so on. Decisions, rules, and guides have in many cases announced new doctrine and modified old. Summarizing this mass of doctrine—much of it obsolete—is no mean task.[1] In the circumstances there is much to be said for proceeding by way of a sample. Since the interest here is not historical, the sample may be taken from the commission's recent activities.

The discussion that follows will consider first all the cases decided by the commission in fiscal year 1963, and then all the cases decided during a six-month period in 1968—chosen because these are the cases reported in the last volume of commission decisions that has been published. Then, using another source, it will consider the commission's output of decisions during the twelve-month period ending June 1, 1973. This procedure will enable us to obtain a fairly representative view of the commission's activities in the past decade.[2] We shall divide our discussion into two parts, bracketing the 1964 and 1968 results and then treating the most recent period separately.

Commission Doctrines and Priorities in the 1960s

Table I classifies the deceptive-practice decisions rendered by the commission in fiscal year 1963.[3] Cases are divided into four categories. Only the last of these, it will appear, represents an appropriate exercise of the commission's authority.

Table 1

FTC DECEPTIVE-PRACTICES DECISIONS, FISCAL YEAR 1963

	Number	Percent of Total
1. Cases not involving serious deception		
Disputes among experts	5	
Collection agencies	4	
Foreign origin	12	
Fictitious pricing	14	
Guarantees	10	
Free	3	
Bait and switch	4	
Other	24	
Subtotal	76	35
2. Cases in which private remedies adequate		
Passing off and disparagement	12	
Sales to businessmen	11	
Fur, wool, and textile fiber acts	69	
Subtotal	92	43
3. Criminal fraud	24	11
4. Appropriate cases for FTC	23	11
Total	215	100

Source: U.S. Federal Trade Commission, *Federal Trade Commission Decisions,* volumes 61, 62.

Category one—cases not involving serious deception—includes, as a subcategory, cases that turn on the resolution of a technical dispute among experts, such as the efficacy of vitamin and iron supplements, the salubriousness of yogurt, the durability of a "six-month" floor wax, and so on. Where, as here, there is a genuine difference of opinion on the merits of a product, any conclusion that the claim for the product is false seems arbitrary. The verdict in such cases should be left to the market. The spirit of the First Amendment would appear to require as much.

Another group of cases within category one involves the practice of collection agencies in smoking out elusive debtors by announcing that a reward or bequest awaits the individual whom they are trying to run to ground.[5] This may or may not be an appropriate creditor's remedy, but certainly no issue of consumer product information is involved.

Other cases involve nondisclosure of the foreign origin of bad-minton-set components, watch bands, and other products.[6] The concern with consumer protection in these cases is a bit attenuated. In one foreign origin case *domestic* manufacturers were called to testify that consumers prefer American-made products.[7] Another decision compelled disclosure of the foreign origin of ball bearings supplied, not to the presumed-to-be-xenophobic consumer, but to manufacturers.[8] In no case was there a suggestion that foreign materials or workmanship were inferior in quality to domestic, or otherwise distinguishable save in being cheaper. These cases appear to have nothing to do with supplying information that consumers require in order to make value-maximizing purchases.

A number of the cases in the first category involve allegations of fictitious pricing. A sale price is represented to be lower than the seller's regular price or the manufacturer's pre-ticketed or list price. The seller's representation is usually accurate. The sale price *is* lower than the former price; the compared price *is* the bona fide manufacturer's list price. The commission's complaint is that the seller did not have many sales at the former price or that, owing to widespread discount selling in the local area, the manufacturer's list price is not a common selling price there.[9] But consumers surely realize that price reductions are commonly motivated by the seller's inability to move the item at the former price and that many products are rarely sold at the manufacturer's list price. These cases appear to serve little purpose other than the harassment of discount sellers.[10]

Among the many other cases in which it is unbelievable that an appreciable number of consumers would be (or even were intended to be) fooled are cases in which the commission orders a seller of dime store jewelry to disclose that its "turquoise" rings do not contain real turquoises,[11] a toy manufacturer to disclose that its toy does not fire projectiles that actually explode,[12] a maker of "First Prize" bobby pins to change the name lest a consumer think that purchase would make him eligible to enter a contest,[13] and a manufacturer of shaving cream to cease representing that his product can shave sandpaper without first soaking the sandpaper for several hours.[14] The representation that a product is "guaranteed" is interpreted by the FTC, but probably not by any consumer, to mean fully guaranteed. The commission deems the term misleading per se unless all the conditions of the guarantee are printed in the ad.[15] "Free"—as in "buy one, get one free"—means to the commission, and only to the commission, a true gratuity.[16]

One may easily find other examples of the commission's proclivity for giving unnatural readings to sales representations.[17] Evidently the commission is unwilling to allow the consumer to shoulder any part of the responsibility for averting unhappy purchas-

19

ing experiences. This is so even in cases where it is plain that the consumer's only effective protection is self-protection.[18] The practice of offering a cheap product in order to get a hearing from the consumer, and then trying to switch the consumer to a more expensive one, is deemed fraudulent even when the seller is prepared to sell the cheaper product if the consumer prefers it.[19]

Category two comprises a large group of the year's consumer-protection cases in which, if there is any fraud, the matter is one appropriately handled by means of private legal remedies, and there is no occasion for an expenditure of public funds. This includes cases of passing off one product as another and of falsely disparaging competitors. Typical are false claims that a product is "stone china"[20] or "whole cowhide"[21] or meets the standards of the Aluminum Window Manufacturers Association.[22] In each case the trade association composed of sellers of the genuine article could have obtained an injunction in a private action.[23]

Other cases in this category involve sales not to consumers but to business purchasers.[24] It might reasonably be assumed that business purchasers should, in general, be held responsible for protecting themselves against deception, either by the exercise of normal caution (which would have averted most of the frauds involved in these cases) or by invoking the contractual remedies on which business enterprises normally rely in purchasing.

The remaining cases in this category, and the vast majority, are cases under the wool, fur, and textile fiber products acts.[25] Sellers of such products who employ fraud could be dealt with under Section 5 of the Federal Trade Commission Act. The purpose of the specialized statutes, as indicated by their terms and their legislative history, is not so much to prevent fraud as to protect the trademarks and goodwill of high-grade furs, wool, and textile fiber products against infringement or dilution by sellers of cheap substitutes.[26] Judging from the cases in the sample, much of the commission's enforcement activity under these statutes consists of springing traps on the unwary. Sellers are convicted for failing to label natural mink "natural,"[27] for using abbreviations instead of the full name,[28] for using the name of an animal in the advertising of a textile product, regardless of disclaimers,[29] although anyone who has ever seen a "fake" (cloth) fur knows that it cannot be mistaken for the real thing, and for other misdeeds of comparable gravity.[30] The main point, however, is not the commission's aberrational enforcement of these curious laws (passed by Congress at the commission's behest),[31] but that the policing of trademarks and quality standards is a job for sellers and their trade associations rather than for the government.

Cases in category three of the sample involve hard-core fraud, where, if the allegations of the complaint be believed, the number and blatancy of the misrepresentations, and sometimes the evasive character of the respondent's operations, indicate the kind of malice or willfulness (in the legal sense of those terms) that would justify criminal proceedings under the federal mail-fraud statute[32] or state criminal fraud laws.[33] These are the freezer-plan, correspondence-school, and other mail-order and door-to-door frauds that have long been a staple of the commission's fraud docket.[34] It would be surprising if the commission, with its highly limited remedial powers, had much impact on fraudulent activity of this sort. The character of the respondents apart, the fraudulent businesses in question require little capital or skill, and entry and exit are rapid. In these circumstances, the threat of a cease-and-desist order has a negligible deterrent effect. If enjoined, the respondent skips nimbly into another line. The commission cannot even force him to disgorge the (often considerable) profits obtained before it struck. Even if the FTC succeeded in placing all currently active con men under order— an objective unlikely to be achieved by the issuance of two dozen orders a year—the effect would be minimal. With entry so easy, others would flood the market.

That leaves only a few cases, some 11 percent of the year's fraud total, in which the commission's action does not appear highly dubious. These include cases where a watch was falsely represented to be shockproof,[35] where the length of a tape was misrepresented,[36] where the interior size of a sleeping bag was misdescribed,[37] and a few others.[38] These are cases where the consumer may have difficulty discovering he has been taken (the watch example is a good one) and where private remedies might be impracticable to pursue, either by consumers or by competing sellers.

In fiscal year 1963, in sum, the FTC bought little consumer protection in exchange for the more than $4 million it expended in the area of fraudulent and unfair marketing practices,[39] and the millions more that it forced the private sector to expend in litigation and compliance. Besides wasting money on red herrings, it inflicted additional social costs of unknown magnitude by impeding the free marketing of cheap substitute products, including foreign products of all kinds, fiber substitutes for animal furs, costume jewelry, and inexpensive scents; by proscribing truthful designations; by harassing discount sellers; by obstructing a fair market test for products of debatable efficacy; and by imposing on sellers the costs of furnishing additional information and on buyers the costs of absorbing that information.

Table 2

FTC DECEPTIVE-PRACTICE DECISIONS,
JULY 1 – DECEMBER 31, 1968

	Number	Percent of Total
1. Cases not involving serious deception		
Collection agencies	3	
Fictitious pricing	6	
Guarantees	6	
Free	1	
Bait and switch	5	
Other	2	
Subtotal	23	19
2. Cases in which private remedies adequate		
Sales to businessmen	11	
Fur, wood, and textile fiber acts	76	
Subtotal	87	71
3. Criminal fraud	9	7
4. Appropriate cases for FTC	4	3
Total	123	100

Source: U.S. Federal Trade Commission, *Federal Trade Commission Decisions,* volume 74.

The 1968 sample presents a similar spectacle of misspent public resources. Table 2 summarizes the decisions in a six-month period, using the same categories as Table 1. As in fiscal year 1963, after subtracting cases in which the deception is trivial, or private remedies adequate, or the commission's powers insufficient to deal effectively with the challenged practice, one finds only a handful of cases in which the commission's intervention seems to have been appropriate.

The subcategory, "sales to businessmen," is dominated by chinchilla cases, wherein people were persuaded to purchase chinchillas on the representation that they would be able to obtain substantial profits from breeding them.[40] This would seem to be an inappropriate area for commission intervention inasmuch as anyone contemplating going into business might ordinarily be charged with making reasonable investigations, and any reasonable investigation would have unmasked the exaggerated claims of the sellers. This is an area where a proper allocation of search costs would require substantial expenditure of time by the purchaser for his reasonable investigation.

But the notion of encouraging buyers' self-protection is one to which the commission has been largely oblivious.

It is admittedly possible to view the chinchilla cases in a somewhat different light: as a deliberate preying upon the greed and gullibility of foolish people. Under this view, the chinchilla seller is a species of con man who should be made liable for his misrepresentations in order to discourage an activity that has no social value. If this is the proper way to look at the cases, it still does not justify FTC intervention. Rather, it shows that the sellers should have been subjected to criminal sanctions. The commission's sanctions are not appropriate for dealing with con men.

Other than the chinchilla cases, the cases in the 1968 sample are quite similar to those in the previous sample. A further discussion of individual cases would not be illuminating.

Recent Developments

We come now to the most recent cases. Table 3 classifies FTC deceptive-practice orders issued between June 1, 1972, and May 31, 1973. In this table, several new subcategories have been added in category one. One is "contests," a subcategory somewhat similar to bait and switch: the consumer is told he has "won" a contest when in fact everyone wins, the purpose of the contest being to lure the consumer into buying some product of the seller's.[41] There is no product misrepresentation: the consumer gets what he pays for. The phony contest is merely an attention-getter. If the practice imposes any harm on anyone, it is trivial.

Another new subcategory is "unsubstantiated." Applying a hitherto unused theory of deception, the commission argues that the making of a claim without adequate substantiation is itself a deceptive practice, even if the claim is true. For example, an automobile manufacturer claims that its car is "more economical." The claim may or may not be true, but at the time of making the claim the manufacturer does not have in his possession sufficient information to convince the commission that it is true.[42]

The appropriateness of this doctrine is open to question.[43] The consumer is interested in whether a claim is true, not in the evidence the seller has collected to support it. If a product claim, although unsubstantiated when made, turns out to be true, the consumer who purchased the product on the strength of the claim suffers no harm. The commission must know this. It would seem, therefore, that the real purpose of the doctrine is to reduce the commission's costs in prosecuting false-advertising cases by shifting the burden of proof

Table 3

FTC DECEPTIVE-PRACTICE DECISIONS, JUNE 1, 1972 – MAY 31, 1973

	Number	Percent of Total
1. Cases not involving serious deception		
Disputes among experts	1	
Collection agencies	4	
Fictitious pricing	10	
Gurantees	8	
Free	2	
Bait and switch	3	
Contests	3	
Unsubstantiated	3	
Truth in Lending	8	
Other	12	
Subtotal	54	47
2. Cases in which private remedies adequate		
Passing off	3	
Sales to businessmen	7	
Fur, wool, and textile fiber acts	19	
Safety	5	
Subtotal	34	29
3. Criminal fraud	19	16
4. Appropriate cases for FTC	9	8
Total	116	100

Source: Commerce Clearing House, *Trade Regulation Reporter,* vol. 3 (1973), paragraphs 20016-20334.

of truthfulness from the commission to the respondent. In itself this might not be unjustifiable if, as is plausible, the pertinent evidence is likely to be more accessible to the advertiser than to the commission. What is disturbing about the substantiation doctrine[44]— if one may judge from the commission's leading decision—is the amount and kind of evidence that the commission will insist that the advertiser collect before making the advertisement.

The commission seems, indeed, to be following the approach taken by Congress in the 1962 New Drug Amendments, which require detailed proof of efficacy before a new drug can lawfully be marketed. There is now evidence that the cost of furnishing proof satisfactory to the Food and Drug Administration has been so great as to force substantial reductions in the number of new drugs being marketed in this country, to the detriment of those who might be helped by them.[45] One can anticipate similar results from the commission's substantiation doctrine. The costs of providing substantiation are apt to discourage the advertising of claims (and hence the marketing of products embodying those claims) that are costly to substantiate. The flow of information to the consumer will be reduced—a result difficult to justify, given the analysis in Section I. It may be observed that the burden of the new policy will fall most heavily on new products and firms. By increasing costs to new entrants the policy will tend to thwart the antitrust policies that the commission is also charged with furthering.

The third subcategory consists of cases brought under the Truth in Lending Act, a recent addition to the statutes enforced by the commission.[46] The act requires detailed disclosure of the terms of credit transactions. In particular, it requires lenders to state the cost of loans in terms of an annual percentage rate of interest. There is serious question whether the information disclosure required by the act is in fact likely to be valuable to the consumer.[47] The consumer is not interested in interest rates as such. He is interested in the total cost of the product he is buying. This will include an interest charge if he is using borrowed money to buy the product. He will therefore purchase from the seller (or the combination of seller and lender) where his total cost, including interest charge, is lowest. But it is the total cost that he is interested in, not the interest component.

It may be assumed for argument that a consumer, shopping for a color television set, is quoted three prices: $450 cash, $20 a month for thirty-six months, and $22 a month for thirty-six months. He knows that if he chooses either the second or third, the total cost will be higher than if he chooses the first. He knows also that if he decides to buy on time, the second is cheaper than the third. He will have to compare the advantage of paying a lower price all at once with the advantage (crucial if he does not have $450) of paying a larger amount in monthly installments. He will not be helped in this comparison by an interest-rate figure unless he is in the habit of saying to himself: "my personal discount rate is ___ percent."

He would, of course, be well advised to find out what a bank would charge him, per month, if he borrowed $450 from it to buy the set for cash; but if he does this, he will still be comparing dollar amounts rather than percentages. He will be guided to the purchase that is optimum from his standpoint, without ever being given an interest-rate figure.

Admittedly, this analysis is oversimplified. It ignores such complications as balloon payments and service charges which may make it difficult for the credit buyer to compare the cost of alternative transactions. (A similar problem is said to plague comparison of life insurance policies.) It may nevertheless be argued that the consumer will normally have all the information he wants without disclosure of a percentage interest rate. If in our example of the color television set, one seller offers terms of $10 a month for twenty-four months, with $600 due the twenty-fifth month, the buyer can readily compute that the total amount he will pay under this plan—$840—is greater than the amounts asked under the alternative plans available to him. He must balance the additional burden against the advantage of a lower monthly payment the first two years. Unless the purchaser is accustomed to thinking in terms of percentage discount rates, a disclosure that the interest rate is higher —or lower—under the balloon-payment plan than under the other plans will not be useful to him.

The residual category of marginal cases in the 1972-1973 sample contains a number of interesting illustrations of the commission's concern with practices not in fact seriously deceptive. One case in this subcategory involves failure to disclose that a candy endorsement by a group of athletes was procured by paying the athletes.[48] Surely very few consumers actually believe that athletes (or other celebrities) endorse products on television without being paid— except of course young children, but they might well respect the endorsement regardless of whether the athlete was paid to make it. A second case involved a claim that a particular type of carton was "biodegradable." The carton had in fact biodegradable characteristics, but it was not completely biodegradable—which is a matter of nuance.[49]

Another case in this group involved a claim that a particular brand of tires had better traction than others. In fact the superior qualities of the tires in stopping a car short had been proved only with respect to wet surfaces.[50] The advertiser pointed out to the commission that, if anything, the advertisement would have been more rather than less effective had it claimed superior traction on wet surfaces. Drivers not only are especially concerned about good tire performance on such surfaces, but would be apt to infer that the tires must also be superior on dry surfaces. In any event, it seems unlikely that many consumers could have been misled by the failure to qualify the claim.

A fourth case involved a disclosure in a mail order house's catalog that "all orders are subject to [firm name]'s credit approval." The commission held that this did not apprise the customer with sufficient clarity that monthly payments must be paid regularly by the customer and that other conditions must be met before credit would be extended.[51] The element of deception is, at the very least, elusive. Everyone knows that conditions such as prompt payment are ordinarily attached to the extension of credit.

In category two (private remedies adequate), we have a new subcategory, "safety." This is made up of cases where the deception concerns the safety characteristics of the product: the seller fails to disclose that a mattress is inflammable, or misrepresents the safety features of a motorcycle helmet. At first glance, these may appear to be especially costly forms of deception and hence particularly suitable for FTC action. But they are cases where private tort remedies would appear perfectly adequate to ensure the customer either the level of safety he wants or compensation for injuries resulting from the seller's failure to supply that level. A person injured by a fire in a mattress that the seller represented to be fire-proof can obtain substantial damages from the seller in a private action. There is no special reason for administrative action.

The "passing off" cases in the sample do not involve passing off in the technical sense in which that term is used in trademark infringement cases. Instead they involve misrepresentations designed to promote a particular product over its close substitutes. In one case, the respondent was a credit card company that misrepresented the potential liability of holders of other credit cards in the event that the cards were lost.[52] In the other two cases in this subcategory the seller of an artificial fruit-juice substitute falsely claimed that his product had all of the qualities of the natural product.[53] In all three cases the burden might reasonably rest with the trade associations of the sellers of the substitute products to dispel the misrepresentation, either by advertising or by legal action against the misrepresenting seller.

An interesting feature of this sample is the sharp decline in the proportion of fur, wool, and textile fiber cases. They constitute only about 10 percent of the cases in the sample, compared with about two-thirds and one-third for 1968 and 1962-1963, respectively. This is consistent with a general increase in the scope and ambition of the commission's activities, an ambition manifest in the amount of doctrinal and remedial innovation in the commission's recent work and in its penchant for suing large firms rather than small, as well as in its de-emphasis of the undramatic, unimportant, and unsuitable enforcement of the specialized statutes. An answer to the question whether greater ambition has resulted in substantially better performance will be suggested later, though the reader may, if he likes, guess at it now.

The nine cases out of 116 that I have classified as apparently appropriate invocations of the commission's power form an interesting collection. They are all cases where the nature of the product and the nature of the claim were such as to make detection of deceptive advertising difficult, but the fraud was not so blatant that criminal remedies would have been feasible or appropriate. In one case, a stimulant was advertised and sold without disclosure that its active ingredient was caffeine.[54] Since most people are familiar with the effects of coffee, this fact would have been informative, and it is information that the consumer could not obtain readily from other sources were it not disclosed by the seller. A similar case involved misrepresentation of the content of bread.[55] Another involved a false claim by the trade association of sugar refiners that taking sugar before meals would facilitate weight reduction.[56] In view of the many different factors that affect weight reduction, it is quite possible that a consumer who followed the advice of the association would not discover for quite a while that the advice was unsound. Furthermore, since the misrepresentation was made on behalf of all sugar refiners, no seller of sugar would have a substantial incentive to take steps to unmask the deception. However, there are close substitutes for sugar for overweight and diabetic people, and the manufacturers of these substitutes might well have strong incentives to take steps to correct the deception.

Another case in this group involved a phony television demonstration, where, again, the consumer was not in a good position to detect the fraud.[57] Yet another involved the practice of a major camera manufacturer in selling returned cameras as new.[58] A consumer would find it difficult to ascertain by inspection that a camera sold as new was in fact used; it might be years before he discovered that the performance of the camera was inferior because it was used.

While some useful cases were brought in the period June 1, 1972, to May 31, 1973, and the number of idiotic cases declined, the overall pattern of commission enforcement does not appear to have differed markedly from that of the earlier periods examined. As before, the bulk of the commission's resources were devoted to marginal cases, to cases where private remedies would probably have been adequate, and to cases where the commission's lack of punitive remedies prevented it from dealing effectively with the challenged practice. In fewer than 10 percent of the cases does the FTC's action appear to have been warranted on the basis of the considerations discussed in Sections I and II.

This conclusion is likely to be challenged on the ground that the sample reveals remedial innovations. It can be argued that these have equipped the commission with sufficiently draconian sanctions to deal effectively even with hard-core criminal frauds. In several cases in the 1972-1973 sample, the commission required the seller to devote a portion of his future advertising to express retraction of the challenged claim;[59] and in one case, the commission ordered the respondent to pay to the bilked consumers the amount he had defrauded them.[60] Unquestionably these remedies strengthen the FTC's sanctions. They impose greater costs on respondents than would be imposed by a simple cease-and-desist order. The threat of their imposition can therefore be expected to deter fraud more effectively than if the commission limited itself to the issuance of simple injunctive orders.

Two questions arise, however. The first is whether the commission has the legal authority to require either "corrective advertising" (as the retraction orders are known) or refunds to defrauded consumers. The answer is "yes" with respect to corrective advertising, because it can always be justified, however factitiously, as necessary to dispel the misleading impact of the respondent's misrepresentations. The courts are likely to uphold the commission's authority to order refunds.[61]

The second question is whether such remedies as corrective advertising and refunds are sufficient to deal with the problem of hard-core or criminal fraud. This is doubtful. Punitive sanctions, which impose on the violator costs greater than the costs of his offense to victims of the particular violation for which he has been apprehended, are necessary to deter this kind of fraud. The commission's recent remedial innovations do not equip it with that kind of punitive sanction.[62]

It may be concluded that even if the commission's recent innovations prove not to be a mere flash in the pan, the commission's resources will continue to be misdirected to a considerable extent.[63]

IV. CONCLUSIONS AND RECOMMENDATIONS

The principal finding of Section III is that only a small fraction of
the Federal Trade Commission's activities in the false-advertising
area is consistent with a proper allocation of commission resources,
considering the character of the false-advertising problem (discussed
in Section I) and the limitations of the commission's sanctions (discussed in Section II). To be sure, it is possible that even though the
commission's constructive activity is very small in any given year,
the very existence of the commission serves to deter a great deal of
unlawful conduct. But it is unlikely that the FTC's power to deter
is very great, given the limitations of its sanctions. And against any
beneficial deterrent effect must be set off at least two costs: the costs
arising from the deterrence of beneficial advertising activity and
the costs of administering the prohibitions enforced by the commission. As to the first, it is obvious from the discussion of the
commission's work product in the sample years that some portion of
the practices enjoined by the FTC do not involve actual deception,
and that in this portion the effect of prohibition is to reduce the flow
of information to the consumer. The direct costs of enforcement
and compliance are also substantial. On balance, one may doubt
whether the benefits from the commission's efforts to prevent false
advertising actually exceed the costs. But since the FTC is unlikely
to be shorn of its false-advertising powers regardless of what a
cost-benefit analysis might show, it may be more practical to concen-
trate on particular deficiencies in the commission's practices, and
how they might be remedied.

The cardinal shortcomings in the commission's false-advertising
endeavors are two. First, the commission has never developed a
theory defining the circumstances under which serious advertising

abuses are likely to occur and where resources should therefore be concentrated. Without such a theory it cannot hope to improve, on average, the functioning of the markets that it regulates. Second, the commission remains oblivious to the severe limitations of its sanctions in relation to those otherwise available. In cases where private remedies are adequate, the commission should have complainants seek those remedies. In cases where the respondent appears to be guilty of criminal fraud, the commission should refer the matter to the appropriate criminal law enforcement authorities for action. *The first priority for the reform of the commission is to develop a theory of consumer fraud and a theory of the place of the FTC's remedies among all remedies available to combat consumer fraud.*

I turn now to possible changes in the legislative framework governing the commission. The most fruitful change within the bounds of feasibility would be to create federal criminal remedies for deliberate consumer fraud. The model for these remedies exists in the federal laws providing criminal penalties for fraud in the sale of securities. The creation of these remedies would eliminate the commission's excuse for continuing to bring cases against "con men," where its remedies seem inadequate, and its justification for stretching the statutory scheme to embrace punitive remedies under other names (corrective advertising, refunds, and so on).

The alternative would be to grant the commission express power to mete out punitive sanctions, but this seems unacceptable. As I have explained elsewhere,[1] it is inappropriate to vest punitive sanctions in a body that cannot be depended upon to judge defendants with complete impartiality. The reason, in brief, is that where sanctions are severe, the costs of their erroneous imposition tend to be quite high. An administrative agency cannot be expected to be wholly free from bias in favor of imposing sanctions in borderline cases, because its performance is likely to be judged by the number of remedial orders that it issues rather than by the impartiality of its processes. In these borderline cases, it may be inclined to err against respondents. These errors would be a source of heavy social costs if the commission were empowered to impose punitive sanctions, which tend to be very costly to those on whom they are imposed.

The creation of a body of federal criminal law applicable to deliberate fraud would enable a better appraisal of the true need for a federal regulatory agency in the false-advertising area. To assist in demarcating that area of the consumer-fraud problem in which such an agency is appropriate, I suggest amending the Federal Trade Commission Act to require that the commission, in issuing any complaint, include a brief statement as to why it thinks private remedies (such as a class action by injured consumers or a suit under the Lanham Act by competitors of the fraudulent seller) would be inadequate to deal with the problem to which the commission's complaint was directed. This reform could of course be implemented by the commission without awaiting legislative action. It is possible —it is, indeed, implied by the survey of the commission's workload given here—that only a small area would remain in which the need for an agency such as the Federal Trade Commission could be demonstrated.

NOTES

NOTE TO INTRODUCTION

[1] For a general description of the commission's functions and powers, see Commerce Clearing House, *Trade Regulation Reporter*, vol. 3 (1973), p. 9500ff. There is a voluminous body of critiques of the FTC, which the reader may (or may not) wish to consult. The major studies, in chronological order, are G. Henderson, *The Federal Trade Commission* (New Haven: Yale University Press, 1924); Commission on Organization of the Executive Branch of the Government, Task Force on Regulatory Commission, *Appendix N* (Washington: U.S. Government Printing Office, 1949); J. Landis, *Report on Regulatory Agencies to the President-Elect* (Washington: U.S. Government Printing Office, 1960); C. Auerbach, "The Federal Trade Commission: Internal Organization and Procedure," *Minnesota Law Review*, vol. 48 (1964), p. 383ff.; E. Cox, R. Fellmeth and J. Schulz, *Nader Report on the Federal Trade Commission* (New York: Richard W. Baron Publishing Co., 1969); R. Posner, "The Federal Trade Commission," *University of Chicago Law Review*, vol. 37 (1969), p. 47ff.; P. Elman, "Administrative Reform of the Federal Trade Commission," *Georgetown Law Journal*, vol. 59 (1971), p. 777ff. I have addressed some of the issues discussed herein in two recent papers. See R. Posner, "Reflections on Consumerism," *University of Chicago Law School Record*, vol. 20, no. 3 (1973), p. 19ff. and "Truth in Advertising: The Role of Government," in Yale Brozen, ed., *Advertising and Society* (Chicago: University of Chicago Press, forthcoming).

NOTES TO SECTION I

[1] The classic analysis of the economics of information, on which I draw in this part of the study, is George J. Stigler, "The Economics of Information," *Journal of Political Economy*, vol. 69 (1961), p. 213ff., reprinted in his *Organization of Industry* (Homewood, Ill.: Richard D. Irwin, Inc., 1968), p. 171ff. An implicit premise of my discussion is that advertising, unless deceptive, has social value. This premise is ably defended in the recent work of Phillip Nelson. See his "Information and Consumer Behavior," *Journal of Political Economy*, vol. 78 (1970), p. 311ff., and "Advertising as Information," *Journal of Political Economy* (forthcoming). The premise has never, to my knowledge, been questioned by the FTC. Since it is outside of the relevant area of debate, I do not discuss it here.

[2] An important but very limited exception is patent rights. And there are others. Nonetheless, the lack of any general protection of property rights in information is clear.

[3] The costs of search are emphasized in Stigler, "Economics of Information."

[4] The distinction between "search" and "experience" goods is emphasized by Phillip Nelson, "Information and Consumer Behavior."

[5] At common law, a competitor did not have standing to challenge false advertising. See American Washboard Co. v. Saginaw Mfg. Co., 103 Fed. 281 (6th Cir. 1900). But Section 43(a) of the Lanham Act appears expressly to confer such standing. See 15 U.S.C. 1125(a) (1970). Nonetheless, few competitors, it appears, utilize this provision—see "Developments in the Law—Competitive Torts," *Harvard Law Review*, vol. 77 (1964), pp. 888, 908—perhaps for the reason discussed immediately below in text.

[6] These problems are discussed in my article, "Oligopoly and the Antitrust

Laws: A Suggested Approach," *Stanford Law Review,* vol. 21 (1969), pp. 1562, 1570-73.

[7] Other tobacco products might be close substitutes, but their producers would be reluctant to advertise that cigarette smoking was dangerous, since many consumers would assume that other tobacco products must also be dangerous to smoke.

[8] Efforts to collect damages for disease allegedly caused by smoking cigarettes have not been markedly successful, but this has been the result of factors such as the difficulty in proving a causal link between smoking and disease and the argument that smokers assume the risk of contracting diseases caused by smoking. These considerations suggest not that tort remedies are inadequate, but that the case for remedial action against the sale of cigarettes may be weaker than commonly supposed.

[9] The incentive to misrepresent the qualities of products whose performance characteristics are difficult to verify is emphasized in M. Darby and E. Karni, "Free Competition and the Optimal Amount of Fraud," *Journal of Law and Economics,* vol. 16 (1973), p. 67ff.

NOTES TO SECTION II

[1] 38 Stat. 717, as amended, 15 U.S.C. 41 (1970).

[2] See G. Henderson, *The Federal Trade Commission,* pp. 34-37, for a concise discussion of the relevant legislative history; also G. Rublee, "The Original Plan and Early History of the Federal Trade Commission," *Proceedings of the Academy of Political Science,* vol. 11 (1926), pp. 666, 669-70ff.

[3] For the early history of the commission see G. Henderson, *The Federal Trade Commission.*

[4] Federal Trade Commission v. Raladam Co., 282 U.S. 643 (1931).

[5] 52 Stat. 111 (Wheeler-Lea Act).

[6] Of course there is a sense—highly attenuated—in which Congress's continued appropriations of funds for the FTC constitutes some sort of approval for its activities.

[7] See 15 U.S.C. 45(a)(6) (1970).

[8] See 15 U.S.C. 45ff. (1970) for the commission's basic procedures, sanctions, and so forth. Some special (and rather minor) powers relating to the advertising of foods, drugs, and cosmetics will not be discussed here.

[9] These rules are listed in Commerce Clearing House, *Trade Regulation Reporter,* vol. 4 (1973), paragraph 38011ff.

[10] The case for the commission's authority is argued in "Statement of Basis and Purpose of Trade Regulation Rule for the Prevention of Unfair or Deceptive Advertising and Labeling in Relation to the Health Hazards of Smoking," *Federal Register,* vol. 29 (1964), p. 8324ff.

[11] Federal Trade Commission v. National Petroleum Retailers Assn., ——— F.2d ——— (D.C. Cir. 1973). The decision may be appealed to the Supreme Court.

[12] These statutes are the Wool Products Labeling Act, 54 Stat. 1128, as amended, 15 U.S.C. 68 (1970); Fur Products Labeling Act, 65 Stat. 175, as amended, 15 U.S.C. 69 (1970); and Textile Fiber Products Identification Act, 72 Stat. 717, as amended, 15 U.S.C. 70 (1970).

[13] Truth in Lending Act, 82 Stat. 146, as amended, 15 U.S.C. 1601 (1970). See also Fair Credit Reporting Act, 84 Stat. 1128, 15 U.S.C. 1681 (1970). Another recently enacted statute enforced by the commission is the Fair Packaging and Labeling Act, 80 Stat. 1296, 15 U.S.C. 1451 (1970). But this act raises special questions involving optimum standardization of weights and measures that are best treated in a separate study.

[14] See, for example, G. Becker, "Crime and Punishment: An Economic Approach," *Journal of Political Economy,* vol. 76 (1968), p. 169ff.

[15] If the respondent violated an order entered by the commission, the commission could use the violation as a basis for seeking an enforcement order from the court of appeals. Violation of that order would expose the respondent to sanctions for contempt of a court order. But there was no sanction for violation of the commission's order as such.

[16] Administrative Procedure Act, 60 Stat. 237 (1946), as amended, 5 U.S.C., primarily § 551-59, 701-06 (1970).

NOTES TO SECTION III

[1] For an effort to do so, see George J. Alexander, *Honesty and Competition* (Syracuse, N.Y.: Syracuse University Press, 1964).

[2] This is true even though the sample includes only cases and not rules. The substantive doctrines found in decisions and in rules are in general the same. It should be emphasized that the cases discussed in this section do not exhaust the commission's consumer-protection work, some of which is not concerned with accuracy in advertising and other sales methods, but with allegedly coercive or immoral sales methods (for example, punchboards).

[3] The discussion of the cases decided during this period borrows liberally from R. Posner, "The Federal Trade Commission," *University of Chicago Law Review,* vol. 37 (1969), pp. 47, 71-77.

[4] See Lanolin, 1-534; Hadacol, 2-65 ("1" indicates volume 61 of the FTC *Decisions,* "2" volume 62; the second number is the page number); Dannon, 1-840; Continental, 2-1064; cf. the tortured efforts to determine "comparable value" in such cases as Nash, 1-596, 606-09, and Gimbel, 1-1051.

[5] National, 1-883; Mosteller, 2-88; Universal, 2-660; Commercial, 2-1330.

[6] See, for example, Recent Games, 1-44; Giant Plastics, 1-179, Fuller, 2-1320.

[7] Baldwin, 1-1345, 1364.

[8] Hoover Ball, 2-1410.

[9] See Leeds, 1-152; Giant, 1-326; Regina, 1-983; Gimbel, 1-1051.

[10] The Giant case, 1-326, illustrates this point nicely. Giant, a retailer in the Washington, D.C., metropolitan area, was forbidden to compare in advertisements the manufacturer's list or suggested retail price with its own sale price. There was no suggestion that Giant had falsified the list price. The objection was that the list price was not the usual sale price in the Washington area. The reason it was not is that discount selling is extraordinarily prevalent in that area. The effect of the decision is to make it more difficult for Giant and other discount retailers to attract customers from neighboring areas in Maryland and Virginia where discount selling is less widespread.

[11] G & G, 2-663.

[12] Marx, 1-269.

[13] Rieser, 1-1378.

[14] Colgate-Palmolive, 2-1269, aff'd, FTC v. Colgate-Palmolive Co., 380 U.S. 374 (1965). The commission also held in that case that the undisclosed use of a "mock-up" in the television advertisement would have been a deceptive practice even if the product had the claimed attribute. This holding is a precursor of the later substantiation doctrine, discussed in the second part of this section.

[15] See, for example, Altheimer & Baer, 1-430; Morse, 1-1078; Silent, 1-1325.

[16] Altheimer & Baer, 1-430; Garland, 1-552; Fairbanks, 1-877.

[17] See, for example, Borg-Erickson, 1-435, 437 ("Lifetime Service Policy" read to mean "respondent will unconditionally service [the product] without charge for the life of the purchaser"); Gimbel, 1-1051, 1065 ("each of the adver-

tisements carries the caveat 'All sizes approximate' . . . a rug 8 feet 7 inches by 11 feet 7 inches in size is not approximately the same size as a 9′ x 12′ rug. The word 'approximate' will perhaps cover an inch or two departure from the norm, but it cannot in this instance stretch to cover five inches"); Pearls, 2-659, 660-61 (ad for "fabulous simulated pearl creation with the priceless look of precious cultured pearls!" held to be representation that product was made of cultured pearls).

[18] A good example of this point is provided by C.D.I., 2-214, where respondent advertised a device falsely claimed to ensure that a woman using the rhythm method of birth control would avoid conception. A woman eager to avoid pregnancy is ill-advised to shop among contraceptives as she would shop among hats, experimenting until she finds one that works. There are some products that should not be bought without first consulting a specialist, in this case a physician, a staff member of a birth-control clinic, or a social worker. The elimination of misrepresentations in contraceptive advertisements will not touch this problem.

[19] Morse, 1-1078; Excel, 1-1119; Wichita, 2-1105.

[20] Harker, 2-1328.

[21] George Frost, 1-517; see also Nash, 1-596; Accurate, 1-1305.

[22] Cal-Tech, 2-93. For other examples of passing off and disparagement cases see Western, 1-272; Barclay, 1-306; Altheimer & Baer, 1-430; Crestmark, 1-739; Hilton, 1-742; Radiator, 1-748; Chemstrand, 1-1134; cf. Hamilton, 1-371; Country Tweeds, 1-1250; U.S. Testing, 1-1312.

[23] See, for example, Federal-Mogul-Bower Bearings, Inc. v. Azoff, 313 F.2d 405 (6th Cir. 1963); Mutation Mink Breeders Assn. v. Lou Nierenberg Corp., 23 F.R.D. 155 (S.D.N.Y. 1959); Advance Music Corp. v. American Tobacco Co., 296 N.Y. 79, 70 N.E.2d 401 (1946); Houston Chronicle Pub. Co. v. Martin, 64 S.W.2d 816 (Tex. Civ. App. 1933).

[24] For example, Robin, 1-450; U.S. Chemical, 1-485; Helene Curtis, 1-510; Pile, 1-1087; C-E-I-R, 1-1468; Aluminous, 2-1048; Cam, 2-1086.

[25] See note 12, supra, Section II.

[26] See *Hearings on H.R. 944 before a Subcommittee of the House Committee on Interstate and Foreign Commerce,* 76th Congress, 1st session, p. 17 (1939); *Hearings on H.R. 169, 5606 and 6524 before a Subcommittee of the House Committee on Interstate and Foreign Commerce,* 85th Congress, 1st session, pp. 22, 38, 42 (1957); *Hearings on H.R. 2321 before House Committee on Interstate and Foreign Commerce,* 82d Congress, 1st session, p. 8 (1951).

[27] For example, Colt, 1-289; Pollock, 1-457; Gorbatenko, 1-1114.

[28] For example, Pfeifers, 1-578.

[29] Elysee, 1-616; Consolidated, 2-113; Fashion, 2-1223. The commission's penchant for misreading advertisements is prominent in these cases. Thus "silky" is interpreted to mean containing silk (Elysee, supra). See also Fabric Shop, 1-463.

[30] Among the other violations are: failure to state the manufacturer's name on the label (Gorbatenko, 1-1114); understatement of wool, overstatement of cheaper fibers (Sacks, 1-226); use of handwriting in labels, and "mingling" of information not required by the statute with required information (Gervitz, 1-74); use of both sides of label (Artel, 1-284).

[31] See, for example, *Hearings on H.R. 2321 before a Subcommittee of the House Committee on Interstate and Foreign Commerce,* 82d Congress, 1st session, p. 8 (1951).

[32] 18 U.S.C. 1341 (1964).

[33] Collected in Note, "The Regulation of Advertising," *Columbia Law Review,* vol. 56 (1956), pp. 1018, 1098-1111. Apart from subjecting the perpetrator to prosecution under special statutes relating to false advertising or sales representations, these practices may sometimes be punishable as larceny.

[34] See, for example, Greater Premium, 1-278; Aluminum Enterprises, 1-293;

Cleland Simpson, 1-472; Hilton, 1-742; American Transportation, 1-962; Midland, 2-39; Belden, 2-849; Kenron Awning, 2-1402.

[35] For example, Emil Braude, 2-1284.

[36] Superior, 1-416.

[37] North Bergen, 1-447; Geotrade, 2-102.

[38] See, for example, Lam Fi, 1-491; Fairbanks, 1-873; Uniforms by Gilson, 2-1263; Volumes in Values, 2-1385. One may count, if one is generously inclined, some twenty-two cases in the residual category of cases in which FTC action conceivably served some purpose, although all are cases where private remedies, in the absence of the FTC, would probably be adequate to eliminate the fraud. Admittedly, the attempt to distinguish these from hard-core fraud cases where criminal remedies seem necessary and appropriate, and from incredible cases where no one is fooled, is somewhat arbitrary.

[39] See 1963 *FTC Annual Report*, p. 31. The existence of a possibly greater deterrent effect to FTC enforcement is discussed in Section IV below.

[40] For example, Central, 4-706; Blue, 4-727. "4" refers to volume 74 of *FTC Decisions*.

[41] For example, Sewing, 20156. The numbers in these citations (footnotes 41 through 60) refer to paragraph numbers in volume 3 of the current Commerce Clearing House *Trade Regulation Reporter*.

[42] For example, Volvo, 20265.

[43] For a biting criticism of it, see Yale Brozen, "The Impact of FTC Advertising Policies in Competition," *Journal of Marketing* (forthcoming).

[44] Pfizer, 20056.

[45] See S. Peltzman, "An Evaluation of Consumer Protection Legislation: The 1962 Drug Amendments," *Journal of Political Economy* (forthcoming).

[46] See note 13, supra, Section II.

[47] R. Posner, "Reflections on Consumerism," *University of Chicago Law School Record*, vol. 20, no. 3 (1973), pp. 19, 22. The discussion that follows borrows from this article. For empirical support for the view advanced here, see F. Angell, "Some Effects of the Truth-in-Lending Legislation," *Journal of Business*, vol 44 (1971), p 78ff.; cf. H. Kripke, "Gesture and Reality in Consumer Credit Reform," *New York University Law Review*, vol. 44 (1969), pp. 1, 7.

[48] Beatrice, 20107.

[49] Ex-Cell-O, 20152.

[50] Firestone, 20112.

[51] Spiegel, 20199.

[52] Credit, 20215.

[53] MCP, 20249; RJR, 20334.

[54] Williams, 20039.

[55] Freihofer, 20133.

[56] Sugar, 20085.

[57] American, 20071.

[58] Eastman, 20082. The remaining cases in this group are Lipton, 20297; Benton, 20303; Rejuvenation, 20304.

[59] The commission's policy on corrective advertising is explained in its opinion in Pfizer, 20056, a case in which the commission decided, however, not to require it.

[60] Universal, 20240.

[61] To date the commission has taken the position that refunds are justified when the retention of the money by the respondent is itself an unfair or deceptive act or practice. In these circumstances the termination of the challenged practice may perhaps be viewed as requiring refund. The commission has not yet claimed the authority to order a respondent to pay damages. This might involve an amount quite different from what the respondent had obtained from the victims of the fraud; damages are usually measured by the cost to the victim of a wrong rather than by the gain to the wrongdoer.

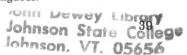

[62] See footnote 61. As mentioned earlier, the proper measure of punitive damages is to divide the victim's actual damages by the probability of the injurer's being apprehended and punished. It is fairly plain that the commission lacks statutory authority to impose monetary sanctions, so measured, on respondents.

[63] It is worth noting that the budget of the commission for consumer protection has increased substantially in recent years, from $4 million in 1962-1963 to $12.5 million in 1970-1971. See 1963 *FTC Annual Report*, p. 31; 1971 *FTC Annual Report*, p. 67.

NOTE TO SECTION IV

[1] R. Posner, "An Economic Approach to Legal Procedure and Judicial Administration," *Journal of Legal Studies*, vol. 2 (1973), pp. 399, 416.